Renewable Sources

A renewable energy source is one that doesn't run out, however much we use. There are certain **processes** that always take place on Earth. Somewhere in the world, the wind is blowing and the Sun is shining. Living things are growing everywhere. Water is on the move in rivers and seas. The layers of rock under our feet pump out heat. These constant processes are sources of renewable energy. We can use them to fuel cars, warm our homes, and make electricity. They will not get used up.

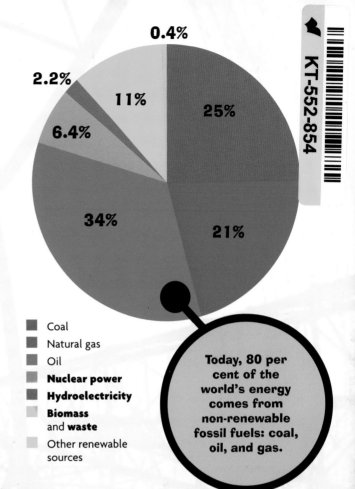

0.4%

2.2%

11%

25%

6.4%

34%

21%

■ Coal
■ Natural gas
■ Oil
■ **Nuclear power**
■ **Hydroelectricity**
■ **Biomass** and **waste**
■ Other renewable sources

Today, 80 per cent of the world's energy comes from non-renewable fossil fuels: coal, oil, and gas.

KT-552-854

Oil use

In 2007 the world produced about 30 billion barrels of oil. Some scientists say we have enough oil left for only 35 years if we use it at this rate. Others say oil will last much longer. They think we will begin to use less oil and more renewable energy.

Climate change

When we burn fossil fuels, they release gases into the air. Some of these gases cause **pollution**. Several of the gases **absorb** the Sun's heat. We call them **greenhouse gases** because they trap heat like a greenhouse (a glass-walled building for growing plants). **Carbon dioxide** is the main greenhouse gas. Others are methane and nitrous oxide. The heat trapped in the **atmosphere** keeps Earth warm and allows life to exist.

We are using such large amounts of fossil fuels that greenhouse gases are increasing. They are putting the world's **climate** out of balance. Scientists have shown that greenhouse gases are causing Earth's climate to change. This change is happening quickly. The world is getting warmer, and weather patterns are changing.

Scientists have linked hurricanes and flooding to climate change. They believe that extreme weather will become more common as the world gets warmer.

How renewables help

To slow climate change, we need to reduce the amounts of fossil fuels we burn. This will reduce the quantity of greenhouse gases in the air. <u>We can use renewable forms of energy that do not increase greenhouse gases</u>. We can make hydroelectricity from water. Underground heat, called **geothermal** energy, can heat our buildings. The heat of the Sun can give us **solar** energy, and the spinning blades of a wind **turbine** (a kind of engine) capture energy from the wind. We can turn these sources of energy into electricity, too.

This **power station** in Denmark makes electricity for 1.3 million households from leftover wood that would otherwise be wasted. Wood is a renewable source of energy because new trees can be planted to replace those used for fuel.

Biomass and biofuels

More than one-tenth of all the fuel we use is **biomass**. Anything that comes from living things is biomass. It includes wood and plant materials. Farming waste, such as dried animal dung, is also biomass. Biomass is a **renewable** source of energy because we can produce more to replace what we use.

Growing and burning

Carbon dioxide is constantly released and **absorbed** by living things. Wood-based fuels could replace **fossil fuels** for some energy needs. If we grow forests to produce the wood we want to burn, we can reduce the amount of carbon dioxide in the **atmosphere**. Some carbon dioxide would always be stored in the growing forests.

1. While trees and other plants grow, they take in carbon dioxide from the air.

2. When wood from trees is burned as fuel, the carbon dioxide is released again.

Inefficient fuel

Biomass is an important energy source in some **developing nations,** where not everyone has electricity. People burn wood and dung to cook food and to keep warm. Open fires are a very **inefficient** (wasteful) way of using fuel. They use a lot of fuel to produce only small amounts of energy. These fires also produce clouds of polluting smoke.

To find out about **biofuels,** turn to the next pages.

Smoke from cooking fires can cause health problems. A better way to use biomass is in **fuel-efficient** stoves. This stove converts more of the fuel's energy into heat than an open fire would.

Biofuels

Biomass can be made into more **efficient** kinds of fuel, called biofuels. They can be used to power vehicles. Some biomass is grown and processed for the purpose of making biofuels. But biofuels can also be made from several kinds of waste. Let's look at some different types of biofuel.

Bioethanol

Brazil grows large amounts of sugar-cane (below). Some of this sugar crop is turned into **bioethanol**. As a fuel, bioethanol produces less **pollution** than petrol. Half of Brazil's cars are powered by bioethanol.

The USA produces bioethanol from corn. Corn bioethanol costs more to produce than sugar-cane bioethanol because the corn has to be turned into sugar before it is processed. Energy and labour costs are higher in the USA, too. So corn bioethanol is not as efficient as sugar-cane bioethanol.

BIOGAS

Biogas can be made from rubbish, animal waste, or **sewage** (waste from bathrooms and kitchens). Once it has been **purified**, or cleaned, it is very similar to natural gas.

In Sweden, more than 7,000 vehicles run on biogas. Some Swedish trains (below) are powered by biogas made from parts of cows not used for food. The waste parts are cooked slowly for a month to extract the gas. Biogas can also be used for cooking and for heating.

Biodiesel

Biodiesel is a biofuel that can be used in **diesel engines**. The diesel engine is named after its German inventor, Rudolf Diesel. He built the first one in 1897. It ran on peanut oil.

Today biofuels are made from other plant oils. In Europe, people make large amounts of biodiesel from rapeseed oil. In the USA, soybeans and vegetable oil are two common sources of biodiesel.

Problems with biofuels

Biofuels are renewable. When burned, they produce less carbon dioxide than fossil fuels. However, many are produced from farm crops. <u>The use of crops for biofuels is affecting the environment</u>. In some countries, rainforests and grasslands are being destroyed to make space for biofuel crops. In other countries, the use of farmland for biofuels is reducing the food supply.

Fat to fuel

In 1998, student Justin Carven developed a system to run his car on used cooking oil. He now has a big factory in the USA making kits that convert lorries and cars to run on used cooking oil.

In North America and Europe, corn, soybeans, and rapeseed are being grown for biofuel. This raises the prices of the crops and makes food more expensive.

In Southeast Asia, farmers are cutting down rainforests and planting coconut trees. The palm oil from them is used to make biodiesel.

In South America, rainforests and grasslands are being cleared to make way for biofuel crops.

In Africa, some farmers grow crops for biofuel instead of food. This can mean there is not enough food to go round.

Biofuels future

There is hope for the future. New kinds of biofuel are being tested. They are made from plants such as switchgrass. **Switchgrass** is not a food and does not need to be grown on farmland. It produces more biofuel per hectare of land than most other plants.

Researchers are also testing biofuels made from **algae** (simple plant-like life forms that grow mostly in water). Growing algae would use less energy and would not take up good farmland.

In 2008, Andy Pag and co-driver Ester Obiri drove 3,750 kilometres (2,330 miles) from London to Athens, Greece. Their car ran on used cooking oil that they got from restaurants along the way.

Hydroelectricity

Any **power station** needs a source of energy to make electricity. <u>Electricity can be made from fossil fuels or from renewable energy sources</u>. In a **hydroelectric power station**, the energy comes from flowing water. This is **kinetic energy** – the energy of movement.

Hydroelectric power

Most hydroelectric power stations are next to a large **dam**. The dam forms a barrier to stop the flowing water of a river. Dams can also increase the head of water (the distance the water falls as it goes through the power station). This makes the water flow stronger. A large **reservoir** forms behind the dam. A reservoir is a store of water that can be used when rainfall is low.

The moving water turns a **turbine**, which is a type of engine powered by a flow of **fluid** (liquid or gas). The spinning turbine turns a **generator**, which is a machine that makes electricity. The picture opposite shows how all this works.

Ancient water-power

Humans have been using water-power for thousands of years. Ancient Greeks used **water-wheels** to grind corn into flour. By AD 31, Chinese people were using water-wheels to pump air and power hammers. In about AD 300, the Romans built a water-powered **mill** that could grind flour for 8,000 people. In the 18th century, water powered all kinds of machinery. These water-powered mills were the first factories.

Wind power and ocean energy also use kinetic energy. Find out more on pages 19-21 and 32-33.

Facts about dams

• There are about 45,000 large dams worldwide. Half of them are in China.

• Hydroelectric plants produce 20 per cent of the world's electricity.

• 40 to 80 million people have had to move out of their homes because the places where they lived were flooded to form reservoirs.

• The world's biggest reservoir is Lake Volta in Ghana. It covers 8,500 square kilometres (3,280 square miles).

In this type of hydroelectric power station, water from the reservoir flows down a narrow tunnel called a penstock. The water flows over the turbine and makes it turn. The turning turbine powers a generator in the powerhouse. The generator produces electricity.

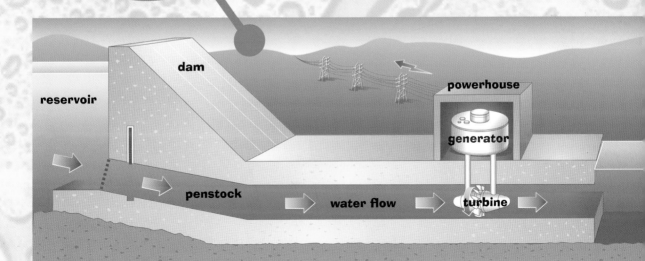

dam

powerhouse

reservoir

generator

penstock

water flow

turbine

Clean and efficient power

The world's water is constantly being recycled. Because of this, <u>hydroelectricity is a renewable form of energy.</u> Water-power is clean. No fuel is burned, so no **carbon dioxide** is produced. It is also **efficient**. A modern turbine can turn 90 per cent of the water's energy into electricity.

Problems and solutions

Big dams can cause serious problems. Large areas of land are flooded when a dam is built. People and wildlife lose their homes.

The river below a power station is changed in several ways. Water that has been stored in a reservoir and then sent through turbines is warmer than water above the dam. This affects the animals and plants that live in and around the river.

The Three Gorges Dam in China is the biggest hydroelectric project in the world. More than one million people lost their homes to make space for the project.

Also, the water flow from a hydroelectric power station is not regular. There may be a sudden rush when the penstocks are opened. Then the water flow falls off again. This can affect the river wildlife.

There is an answer to some of the problems that hydroelectric projects cause. Hydroelectricity can be produced on a small scale with micro-hydro systems. "Micro" means small, and small turbines don't need dams. Many small turbines together can produce as much electricity as a large power station.

BRIGHT IDEA

Stream power

Ian Gilmartin and Bob Cattley from Cumbria in the UK have invented a micro-hydro system. It uses a new type of small-scale water-wheel. The system provides energy from a head of just 20 centimetres (8 inches). In a small stream, it can provide enough electricity to power a house.

Micro-hydro systems are simple to build and run. The systems channel water from a stream or river into a small turbine. This type of system can provide a village with power for lighting and cooking.

WIND POWER

When the wind blows, it creates **kinetic energy. If kinetic energy is captured, it can be turned into other forms of energy.** Wind is a **renewable** source of energy because it never runs out. It is clean because it does not produce **pollution** or **carbon dioxide.**

Windmills in history

Windmills have been used to mill (or grind) flour for more than one thousand years. The first windmills were probably built in Central Asia in the 9th century. Hundreds of years later, people began using windmills to pump water out of the ground.

Until the middle of the 20th century, many farms and ranches in the USA used windmills to pump water out of the ground. Windmills are still used to pump water in places where there is no electric power.

18

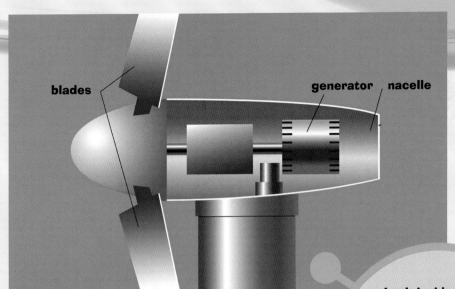

blades   generator   nacelle

Capturing and converting energy

Windmills are machines that convert (change) the wind's movement into the power to move machinery. A wind **turbine** is a type of windmill that produces electricity. It has blades to catch the wind. The turbine converts the movement of the air into power for a **generator**. The generator uses that power to make electricity.

Look inside a wind turbine: the case around the generator is called the nacelle. The blades are mounted near the tip of the nacelle. The nacelle can turn so the blades face the wind. As the blades spin, they power the generator.

Producing power

Large wind turbines are very powerful. The biggest turbines can produce enough electricity for 1,500 to 5,000 households.

Power stations using wind can be big or small. Some have a single turbine, while others may have hundreds. These large power stations, called wind farms, are cheap to build compared to other power stations.

Wind challenges

What happens when the wind stops blowing? One problem with wind power is that the wind does not blow all the time. Another is that the wind can blow fast or slowly. Wind farms must be put in places where there are strong winds a lot of the time.

Other problems

Wind power does have other **disadvantages**. A power station that runs on **fossil fuels** takes up far less space than a wind farm producing the same amount of energy. Wind turbines are often on hills, and many people do not like how they look. People living near a wind turbine also sometimes complain about the noise it makes.

BRIGHT IDEA

Power tower

A new building in China uses the wind to generate its own power. The Pearl River Tower in Guangzhou has openings in its sides to let in breezes. Inside, two turbines catch the wind and turn it into energy for heating and air-conditioning.

Offshore wind farms are probably the best way to capture wind power. The wind at sea is more reliable, and the turbines cannot be heard or seen so easily. Offshore wind farms are expensive to build, however.

Fast and slow

A wind turbine needs wind speeds of 14.5 kilometres per hour (9 miles per hour) to turn. If the wind blows faster than 100 kilometres per hour (62 miles per hour), turbines will shut down so they don't get damaged.

Dangerous skies

Wind turbines can easily kill birds and bats. Planners try not to put wind farms in paths of migrating birds.

In areas with plenty of wind, micro (small) wind turbines are a good way to save on electricity costs. They can provide enough power for one home.

Solar power

The Sun is a ball of fiery gases that release immense amounts of energy. <u>The Sun's energy provides Earth with energy in the form of light and heat.</u> The Sun's heat drives the wind and ocean currents. <u>Plants make food using energy from the Sun, and animals rely on these plants for food.</u>

People today use **solar** energy in many ways. One way is to use the heating effect of the Sun. Another is to make electricity from sunlight. Both these forms of solar energy are **renewable**.

Huge arrays of solar panels provide electricity for the International Space Station.

These houses face south to take advantage of the Sun's thermal energy. Solar panels on their roofs produce electricity from the Sun's light.

Thermal energy

Every day, **thermal** energy (energy from heat) reaches Earth from the Sun. It warms buildings and other objects. This is called passive (unmoving) solar power. People have always used this energy for warmth.

Active solar power systems use pumps or fans to move heat around. They also use panels to collect the Sun's heat. Dark panels with pipes running through them are set up in a sunny place. The panels **absorb** the heat and **transfer** (move) it to liquid in the pipes. The hot liquid can be used to heat a building or a tank of water.

Thermal power stations

Solar thermal **power stations** make electricity from the Sun's heat. They use mirrors to capture sunlight over a large area and focus it on a small area. The focused sunlight is hot enough to turn water into steam. This can drive steam **turbines** and generate electricity.

Some photovoltaic power stations stretch across many hectares of land. This solar power station is in Germany.

Solar cells

Photovoltaic energy is electricity made from light. Solar cells are devices that use photovoltaic energy. They soak up energy from sunlight and turn it into electricity. Solar cells can be used to power a small gadget, such as a personal media player. They can be combined into large panels to produce electricity in a power station. Solar cells are expensive to make. If more people buy them, however, they will become cheaper.

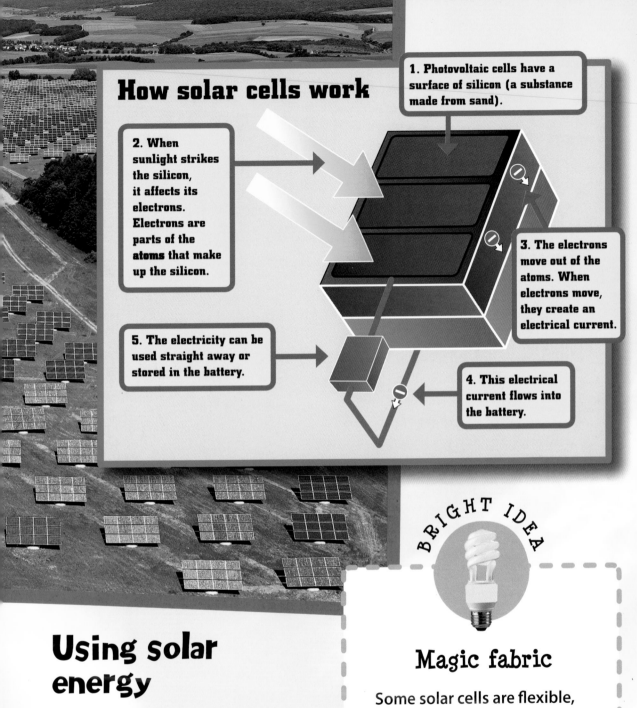

How solar cells work

1. Photovoltaic cells have a surface of silicon (a substance made from sand).

2. When sunlight strikes the silicon, it affects its electrons. Electrons are parts of the **atoms** that make up the silicon.

3. The electrons move out of the atoms. When electrons move, they create an electrical current.

4. This electrical current flows into the battery.

5. The electricity can be used straight away or stored in the battery.

Using solar energy

Solar energy is very **adaptable** and can be used on a large or small scale. It is especially useful in sunny countries and remote places. But no energy can be produced at night and very little on cloudy days.

Magic fabric

Some solar cells are flexible, like fabric. The US Army has used solar fabric for tents. The fabric provides power for lighting and cooling systems inside the tents.

Solar ovens

Solar ovens are boxes that use the Sun's heat to cook food. They use reflectors, or panels that reflect the Sun onto the box to increase the heat.

Solar ovens are useful in sunny places where people have no other power for cooking. They are healthier to use than firewood, and fewer trees get cut down. Solar ovens do not always work, however. In many places, people work in the day and cook in the evening. The solar ovens are not much use after the Sun goes down!

Healthy water

Solar ovens can be used to **purify** (clean) water. Heating water in a solar oven above 71°C (160°F) gets rid of dangerous germs.

People in Bolivia use solar ovens made with wood and glass.

Make a pizza box solar oven

You will need:
- a shallow box with a lid (a pizza box is good)
- a ruler, a pencil, scissors, glue, and tape
- black paint
- aluminium foil
- a sheet of clear plastic
- a stick or drinking straw

Curved cookers

A parabolic solar cooker looks like a satellite dish. It uses its curved shape to reflect heat onto a cooking pot at its focus, or centre.

1. Mark out a square on the box lid, 2–3 centimetres (about 1 inch) in from the edges.

2. Cut round three sides of the square, to make a flap that opens outwards.

3. Tape clear plastic over the gap left in the lid.

4. Glue a layer of aluminium foil to the inside of the flap to make a reflector.

5. Paint the inside of the box black.

6. On a sunny day, wedge the flap open with a straw or stick. Turn your solar oven to face the Sun so it is reflected into your oven. Find and test a recipe from a solar cooking website. **Be careful – your food and dish may get as hot as it does in your kitchen oven!**

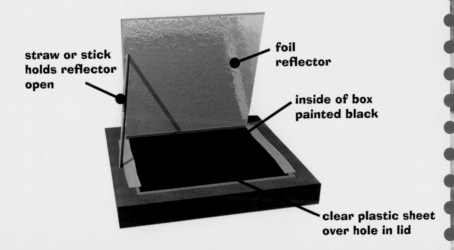

straw or stick holds reflector open

foil reflector

inside of box painted black

clear plastic sheet over hole in lid

Geothermal energy

The word *geothermal* means "heat from the ground". <u>Geothermal energy is energy that comes from inside Earth.</u>

Deep underground, Earth is far hotter than at the surface. This is a constant, natural source of heat that cannot be used up. In a few places, called hot spots, this heat comes close to the surface. We can use the heat found at hot spots to produce geothermal energy.

Geothermal water sometimes comes to the surface by itself. Geysers (spouts of water) and hot springs are formed from geothermal water.

The Svartsengi geothermal power station in Iceland uses a **combined heat and power** system. It makes electricity as well as supplying heat to buildings. The plant's geothermal water has also been used to make a swimming lake.

Drawing heat from the ground

In some places, hot water or steam flows up to the surface by itself and forms hot springs. In other places, engineers drill a deep hole to reach a supply of natural hot water or steam. The hot **fluid** then flows or is pumped up to the surface through a long pipe. This geothermal water or steam can be used for heating.

In a **power station**, <u>heat energy can be turned into electrical energy</u>. Geothermal water or steam is converted into electricity by a **turbine** and a **generator**.

CLEAN CAPITAL

Iceland is in a geothermal area. About 90 per cent of Icelanders use geothermal energy. Since 1930, Iceland's capital Reykjavik has had a geothermal heating system. Geothermal energy does not cause **pollution**. Reykjavik is one of the cleanest cities in the world because of its geothermal heat.

Deep heat

Geothermal energy supplies less than 1 per cent of all our energy needs. This is because there are few places where heat is close to the surface. However, there is much more heat deep in underground rocks. Several kilometres below Earth's surface, the rocks can be as hot as 200 ºC (392 ºF).

Engineers are developing ways to draw this heat from deep inside Earth. They are using **enhanced geothermal systems (EGS)** to do this.

Some EGS power stations have already been built. One enhanced system is called "hot dry-rock". You can see how this works on the opposite page. Cold water is pumped down into cracks in the hot rocks. Once the water has been heated, it is pumped back up to the surface.

BRIGHT IDEA

Warm waters

Many fish grow faster when they are warm. Some fish farms use geothermal water as a source of heat.

Heat pumps

Above ground, temperatures change from hot to cold depending on location and time of year. Just a few metres below ground, the temperature stays at about 10ºC (50ºF) all year round. A geothermal heat pump can use the difference between underground and surface temperatures to heat buildings in winter and cool them in summer. It uses **heat exchange,** or the **transfer** of heat from one area to another.

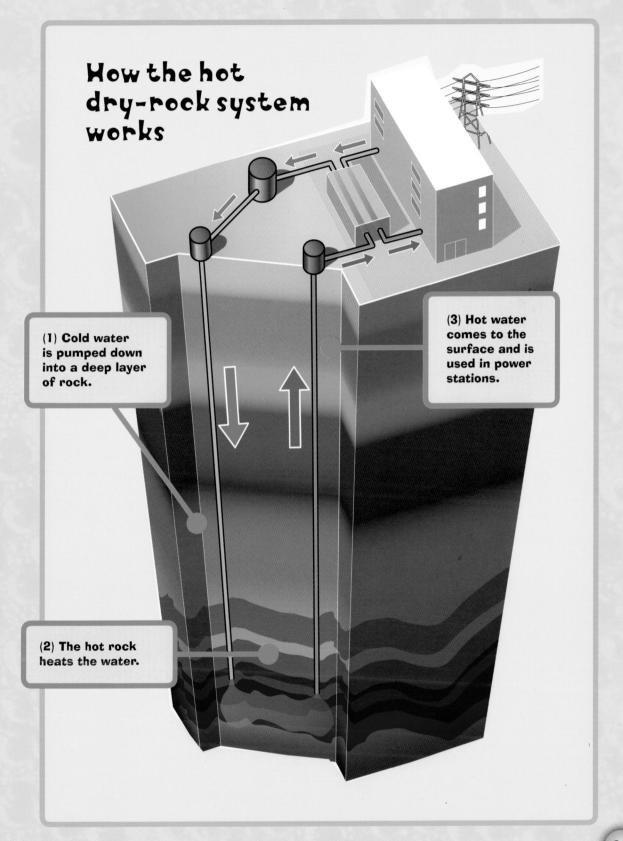

How the hot dry-rock system works

(1) Cold water is pumped down into a deep layer of rock.

(2) The hot rock heats the water.

(3) Hot water comes to the surface and is used in power stations.

Energy in the ocean

Around the world, the water of the oceans is always on the move. The movement of such a huge volume of water contains a lot of **kinetic energy**. It is a **renewable** source of energy because the water never stops moving.

The Pelamis wave energy machine looks like a giant snake. It uses the movement of waves to pump **fluid** to a turbine. The turbine drives a **generator** to make electricity.

Tidal power

Ocean tides rise and fall twice a day along most coasts. This energy in this regular flow of water can be turned into electricity in some places. A tidal **power station** needs a change of 5 metres (16 feet) in the water level between low and high tide. There are only a few places in the world where the tide rises and falls enough. At the La Rance tidal power station in France, a barrage (barrier) stretches right across the mouth of the bay. When the tide goes in or out, water flows through the barrier and turns the **turbines** that make electricity.

Salter's Duck

In the 1970s, Professor Stephen Salter in the UK invented a device to make electricity from the movement of waves. It bobbed up and down on the waves like a duck, so it was called "Salter's Duck". It is very efficient but too expensive to use widely.

Wave power

Tides happens along the coast, but there are waves all over the sea. Waves could supply a huge amount of energy. However, wave power is one of the least developed types of renewable energy.

There are many different wave power ideas being tested around the world. Some float on the waves, while others are fixed to the sea bed. None of these designs has yet been developed into a working power source. So far, these systems are not **efficient** or cheap enough.

On page 44, you'll find a chart that shows the advantages and disadvantages of all the energy sources you are learning about.

Hydrogen fuel

Hydrogen is a very light gas. It is highly flammable, which means it burns easily. Because of this, hydrogen has to be handled carefully, but it makes a good fuel.

When hydrogen burns, it produces no **carbon dioxide**. It is also a clean fuel: the only **waste** product is water. Hydrogen can also be used to make electricity.

On Earth, hydrogen is part of water and many other things. In the universe, it is the most common element (basic substance). Floating in space are huge clouds of hydrogen, such as the ones shown here.

Storage problems

Hydrogen is not easy to store or transport. The gas easily leaks through the smallest hole. Pipelines, pumps, and storage tanks have to be super-airtight.

Making hydrogen

Hydrogen cannot be dug or drilled from the ground like **fossil fuels**. It has to be made, which takes energy. The world produces about 50 million tonnes (55 million tons) of hydrogen every year. The problem is that most of this hydrogen is made using fossil fuels. Making hydrogen this way uses energy and produces large amounts of carbon dioxide. We can make hydrogen from water instead. Water contains plenty of hydrogen, and it is a **resource** that is **renewable**. Water can be split into hydrogen and oxygen. This process is called electrolysis. However, the electrolysis of water uses large amounts of electricity. The process is still very expensive, but people are trying to find ways to bring the cost down. Then hydrogen will become a great alternative (another option) to fossil fuels.

Hydrogen can be burned as a fuel for vehicles, just like petrol. Cars can refuel at hydrogen filling stations like this one.

Fuel cells

A fuel cell is a device that makes electricity from hydrogen. It uses chemical reactions (or changes) to do this. The chemical reaction inside a fuel cell creates an electric current. The electricity from fuel cells can be used to power vehicles. It can also be used to provide electricity in buildings.

Fuel cells have been tested as a power supply for cars and for producing electricity. At present they are expensive to make. If they are produced in large numbers, the price will come down.

In spite of the cost, people in several countries are trying out hydrogen-powered vehicles. In 2010, hydrogen-powered buses will take people to and from the Winter Olympics in Canada.

This fuel cell makes electricity from hydrogen fuel. It can be used instead of a petrol-burning engine to power a car.

Hydrogen hero

US scientist Geoffrey Ballard (1932–2008) developed a widely used fuel cell. He was named a "Hero for the Planet" by *Time* magazine in 1999 for his achievement.

Algae Energy

Algae that grow on the surface of ponds produce small amounts of hydrogen. When US scientists changed the chemicals in pond water, the algae produced more hydrogen. In the future, algae farms may produce hydrogen on a large scale.

PAC-Car II is the world's most **fuel-efficient** vehicle. It is powered by a small hydrogen fuel cell. PAC-Car II can run for 5,385 kilometres (3,346 miles) on an amount of hydrogen equal to 1 litre (0.22 gallons) of petrol.

Nuclear power

Nuclear power is a form of energy that can be made in huge quantities. It does not produce greenhouse gases. But nuclear power has other problems. Today's nuclear power uses uranium (a kind of metal) for fuel. Uranium supplies will probably run out in a few hundred years, so the nuclear power we use today is not renewable. Future forms of nuclear power may be renewable.

The power in the atom

Everything in the world is made up of tiny parts called **atoms**. Inside the atom is a smaller part called the **nucleus**. <u>Nuclear energy is produced when the nucleus is changed</u>. This change is called a nuclear reaction. The reaction used to create nuclear power is known as nuclear **fission**, or splitting, because the nucleus of the atom splits. Nuclear **power stations** produce energy by splitting atoms inside a container called a **reactor**. Then they turn this energy into electricity.

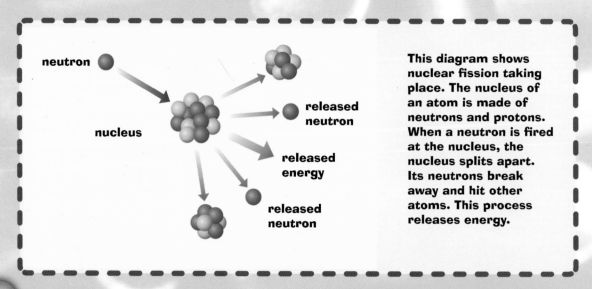

neutron

nucleus

released neutron

released energy

released neutron

This diagram shows nuclear fission taking place. The nucleus of an atom is made of neutrons and protons. When a neutron is fired at the nucleus, the nucleus splits apart. Its neutrons break away and hit other atoms. This process releases energy.

Uranium is made into small pellets to be used for fuel.

Once the **process** has started, it will keep going if there is enough fuel. This **chain reaction** can produce enormous amounts of energy in the form of heat.

Radiation

Nuclear power is energy released in the form of heat. Heat is a kind of **radiation**, which is energy given off in invisible waves, or **rays**. Some forms of radiation can be harmful. Uranium naturally gives off rays that can be dangerous. Substances that give off dangerous rays are called **radioactive**. Harmful radiation can cause people and other living things to get sick or die.

BRIGHT IDEA

Releasing energy

Lise Meitner (1878–1968) was a scientist in Germany in the days when very few women had the opportunity to study science. She was the first person to understand how energy could be released by splitting atoms. Meitner named this process "nuclear fission".

39

Nuclear dangers

When nuclear fission takes place, it gives off large amounts of radiation. That radiation must be contained because it is so dangerous. Engineers carefully control the reactions taking place inside the reactor. The **waste** from nuclear power stations is stored in tight containers to prevent leaks of radiation.

Today, about 6 per cent of the world's energy comes from nuclear fission. Many people are worried about plans to build more nuclear power stations. They say the dangers of using nuclear power are too great.

In this power station, a nuclear reactor creates energy that turns water into steam. The steam turns **turbines** that make electricity.

New reactors

Scientists are looking for ways to build safer nuclear power stations. They are addressing other questions about nuclear power, too. New kinds of reactors may solve several problems. A breeder reactor will recycle uranium. In fact, it will breed, or make, more fuel than it uses.

Nuclear fusion

Fission is only one kind of nuclear reaction. Another is nuclear fusion (joining together). Nuclear fusion happens when **nuclei** join together. This is the way that the Sun produces heat and light. The process could produce huge amounts of energy on Earth.

Nuclear fusion creates less radioactive material than fission. It uses hydrogen as its fuel, and so it is endlessly renewable. But many nuclear scientists say it will be at least fifty years before they can produce safe fusion power.

Future fuel

In the future, the metal thorium could replace uranium as a source of fuel for nuclear power. It is more abundant (available in larger quantities) than uranium. It also produces much less radioactive waste.

Radioactive waste from nuclear power stations must be carefully handled. It is transported and stored in tightly sealed containers.

INTO the FUTURE

No single renewable energy source will replace fossil fuels. We will need to use a mix of renewable sources to meet growing energy needs in the future.

Some renewable energy sources are good for supplying large **power stations**. But we will also use more small-scale energy. More people will have **windmills** and **solar** panels at their homes.

Sky high energy

In the future, we may see wind **turbines** that fly like kites. A turbine high in the sky could make 250 times more energy than one on the ground. It would send electricity to Earth through cables attached to the ground.

Saving energy and working together

All renewable energy sources have great **potential** (promise for the future). Will renewable energy solve the problem of energy supplies? It is hard to tell. One thing is sure: fossil fuels will not be completely replaced for many years. Today, renewable energy only supplies a small fraction of our total energy.

It is important to conserve the energy we have. People are finding more ways to save energy and use fuel more **efficiently**. No one nation or area can solve energy problems by itself. To find good solutions, people are working together and making plans for the future.

Storage solution

Wind power and solar power are not produced in a steady stream. A big challenge for scientists is how to store the energy they produce and then deliver it on demand. As we start to use more renewable power, the problem of storage will grow.

Australian scientist Maria Skyllas-Kazacos invented the flow battery to try and solve the problem. The battery can store energy in liquid chemicals and release it on demand. Skyllas-Kazacos and others are working to make the battery affordable for the future.

It is unlikely that we will ever run out of rubbish. Several methods are being developed to turn **waste** of all kinds into fuel for the future.

ENERGY REVIEW

ENERGY	ADVANTAGES	DISADVANTAGES
Biomass (pages 8–9)	• Open fires require no equipment. • Energy-efficient stoves reduce **pollution** and amount of fuel used.	• Open fires use fuel in an **inefficient** way. • Burning produces polluting smoke and gases. • Growing **biomass** crops has led to forests being cut down.
Biofuels (pages 10–13)	• Less toxic and cleaner than **fossil fuels**. • Can be made from **waste** or from non-food crops.	• **Biofuels** made from food crops use up land and cause food prices to rise. • Growing biofuels produces significant amounts of **carbon dioxide**.
Hydroelectricity (pages 14–17)	• Produces constant energy 24 hours a day. • Causes no pollution.	• **Dams** are very expensive to build. • Dams damage environment, wildlife, and water supplies. • People are moved from their homes to make way for dams.
Wind (pages 18–21)	• Wind **turbines** on land are easy to build. • Cheap to produce and causes no pollution.	• Turbines only make energy when wind blows. • Turbines are noisy and require large areas of land.
Solar (pages 22–27)	• **Adaptable** to small-scale use or in large **power stations**. • Clean form of energy that causes no pollution.	• **Solar** cells are expensive to use because they are not very **efficient**. • Only works well in sunny places.
Geothermal (pages 28–31)	• Produces constant energy 24 hours a day. • Clean form of energy that causes little pollution.	• **Geothermal** water is available only in a few places. • Deep rock energy will require expensive new technology.
Ocean (tidal and wave) (pages 32–33)	• Potentially powerful energy source. • Clean form of energy that causes no pollution.	• Can only be used in certain areas. • New technology is expensive and not yet fully tested.
Hydrogen fuel (pages 34–37)	• Very efficient fuel • Clean form of energy that causes no pollution.	• Current production of hydrogen is either expensive or inefficient. • Hydrogen fuel cells are very expensive.
Nuclear (pages 38–41)	• Clean form of energy with no carbon dioxide emissions. • Produces huge amounts of constant energy 24 hours a day.	• Power stations are very expensive. • **Radiation** is very harmful to all living things. • Supplies of uranium will eventually run out. • Storage of **radioactive** waste is unsolved.

Glossary

absorb take in

adaptable able to be used in different ways

algae simple, plant-like life forms that live in water and have no roots or seeds

atmosphere layer of gases that surrounds Earth and other planets

atoms small pieces of matter that everything else is made up of

biodiesel oil-based fuel made from plant matter

bioethanol alcohol-based fuel made from biomass

biofuel fuel made from biomass

biogas methane-based fuel made from biomass

biomass all matter that comes from living things, including wood and plant materials

carbon dioxide gas composed of carbon and oxygen

chain reaction reaction in which one action causes the next one in a continuous chain

climate overall weather patterns of a region over a long time

combined heat and power system that produces electricity and thermal energy from the same source by recycling waste heat

dam barrier across a body of water that can be used to form a reservoir

developing nation country that is starting to consume more energy and build industries

diesel engine engine that uses compressed air mixed with an oil-based fuel

disadvantage factor that makes something less useful

efficient producing results with little waste of energy

enhanced geothermal system (EGS) geothermal energy system that produces heat and electricity by using the very high temperatures found in hot rock deep below Earth's surface

fission splitting apart

fluid gas or liquid

fossil fuels fuels, including coal, natural gas, and petroleum (oil), that contain carbon and were formed underground from plant and animal matter

fuel-efficient device or system that uses fuel well, with little waste

generator machine that produces electrical energy from kinetic (movement) energy

geothermal using or producing heat energy from the ground

greenhouse gas gas in the atmosphere that traps heat

heat exchange system of transferring heat from one substance or area to another that is used for heating or cooling

hydroelectricity electricity produced from the energy of moving water

inefficient wasteful of energy or not able to work well

kinetic energy energy that comes from movement, such as energy from wind

mill process that grinds or crushes materials; and a factory that uses machines to make things

nuclear power energy produced from a nuclear reaction

nuclei plural of nucleus

nucleus core or centre of an atom

parabolic curved in the shape of a shallow bowl

photovoltaic able to create electrical energy from light

pollution act of damaging air, water, or land with chemicals

potential future possibility or promise

power station place where generators are used to make electricity

process series of actions that continue to happen, such as the wind blowing or plants growing

purify make clean or pure

radiation energy given off by atoms as invisible waves or particles

radioactive able to give off radiation

ray beam or line of radiant energy

reactor place where controlled nuclear reactions take place

renewable able to be replaced

reservoir store of water

resources useful things, such as fuels or materials

sewage waste and dirty water from households and industries that is carried away in sewers

solar coming from the Sun

switchgrass tall, tough type of grass that can grow well even in poor conditions

thermal caused by or relating to heat

transfer move from one place to another, as in heat exchange

turbine machine powered by a flow of fluid. The fluid spins the turbine's moving parts to create mechanical energy.

waste materials that are thrown away, not used, or left over

water-wheel wheel turned by the power of moving water and used to power machinery

windmill machine powered by the energy of the wind

Find out more

Books

Chain Reactions: From Steam Engines to Nuclear Fusion – Discovering Energy, Carol Ballard (Heinemann, 2007)

Energy Essentials: Renewable Energy, Nigel Saunders and Steven Chapman (Raintree, 2004)

Energy Sources: Wind Power, Neil Morris (Franklin Watts, 2008)

Green Files: Future Power, Steve Parker (Heinemann Library, 2004)

New Technology: Energy Technology, Chris Oxlade (Evans Brothers, 2008)

Potato Clocks and Solar Cars: Renewable and Nonrenewable Energy, Elizabeth Raum (Raintree, 2007)

Websites

www.ctgpc.com/pictures/pictures_a.php
China Three Gorges Project
Look at amazing photos of this huge engineering project.

www.eia.doe.gov/kids/energyfacts/sources/renewable/geothermal.html
Geothermal Energy
Find out more about the different uses of geothermal energy.

www.emec.org.uk/tidal_devices.asp
European Marine Energy Centre
See many different wave and tidal devices in action.

www.solarovens.org/recipes/index.html
Recipes for Solar Ovens and Solar Cookers
Try out these recipes in your solar oven!

www.windpower.org/en/kids/index.htm
Wind with Miller
A great guide to wind power.

www.wvic.com/how-gen-works.htm
How an Electric Generator Works
Watch this animation of a generator making electricity.

Index